MALCOLM A TO X

MALCOLM A TO X

The Man and His Ideas

Compiled by David Gallen

Carroll & Graf Publishers, Inc.
New York

Permissions

The publisher gratefully acknowledges permission to reprint from the following:

The Estate of James Baldwin, for excerpts from "Martin and Malcolm" (*Esquire*, April 1972).

Beacon Press, for excerpts from the June 1963 interview between Dr. Kenneth Clark and Malcolm X, which initially appeared in *The Negro Protest* (Beacon Press 1963).

HarperCollins Publishers, Inc., for excerpts from *The Death and Life of Malcolm X* by Peter Goldman (Harper and Row, 1973).

William Kunstler, for excerpts from his 1960 WMCA radio interview with Malcolm X.

Claude Lewis, for excerpts from his December 1964 interview with Malcolm X.

Playboy Enterprises, Inc., for excerpts from the Alex Haley interview with Malcolm X (*Playboy*, May 1963).

A.B. Spellman, for excerpts from his May 1964 interview with Malcolm X (*Revolution*, July/August 1964).

William Morris Agency, Inc., on behalf of the Estate of Robert Penn Warren, for excerpts from his essay "Malcolm X: Mission and Meaning," which initially appeared in *Yale Review* (December 1966); and for excerpts from the Robert Penn Warren interview with Malcolm X, which initially appeared in *Who Speaks for the Negro?* by Robert Penn Warren (Random House, 1965).

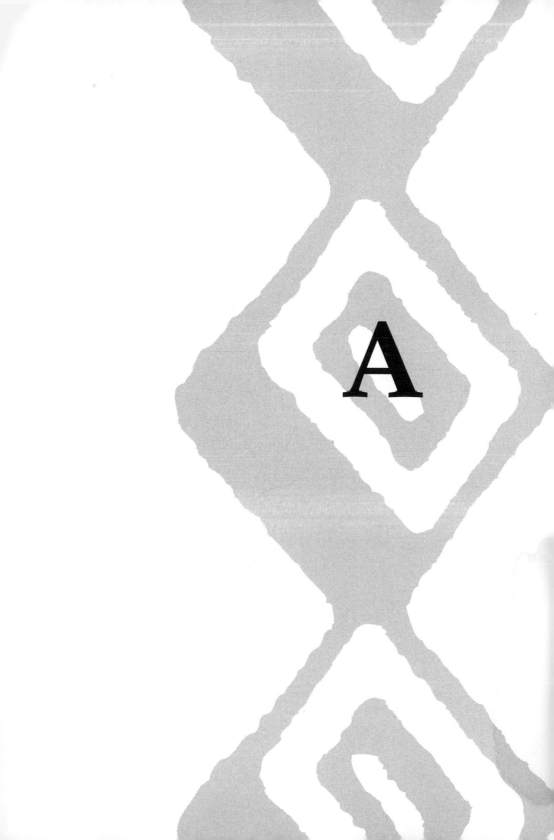

A

A

AGAINST ALL ODDS

i

[Malcolm X] was a latter-day example of an old-fashioned type of American celebrated in grammar school readers, commencement addresses, and speeches at Rotary Club lunches—the man who "makes it," the man who, from humble origins and with meager education, converts, by will, intelligence, and sterling character, his liabilities into assets. Malcolm X was of that breed of Americans, autodidacts and homemade successes, that has included Benjamin Franklin, Abraham Lincoln, P.T. Barnum, Thomas Alva Edison, Booker T. Washington, Mark Twain, Henry Ford, and the Wright Brothers. . . .

Malcolm X (1925–1965),
at Harlem rally in 1963.

UPI/Bettmann Newsphotos

President Abraham Lincoln
(1809–1865).

The Bettmann Archive

The Bettmann Archive

Author Samuel Langhorne
Clemens (1835–1910), better
known by his pen name
Mark Twain.

Booker T. Washington
(1856–1915), educator and
founder of Tuskegee Institute,
in 1903. *The Bettmann Archive*

Furthermore, to round out his American story and insure his fame, Malcolm X, like John Brown, Abraham Lincoln, Joseph Smith (the founder of Mormonism), and John Fitzgerald Kennedy, along with a host of lesser prophets, crowned his mission with martyrdom. Malcolm X fulfills, it would seem, all the requirements—success against odds, the role of the prophet, and martyrdom—for inclusion in the American pantheon.

—Robert Penn Warren (December 1966)

At the bottom of the social heap is the black man in the big-city ghetto. He lives night and day with the rats and cockroaches and drowns himself with alcohol and anesthetizes himself with dope, to try and forget where and what he is. That Negro has given up all hope. He's the hardest one for us to reach, because he's the deepest in the mud. But when you get him, you've got the best kind of Muslim. Because he makes the most drastic change. He's the most fearless. He will stand the longest. He has nothing to lose, not even his life, because he didn't have that in the first place. I look upon myself as a prime example of this category—and as graphic an example as you could find of the salvation of the black man.✓

—Malcolm, the Playboy interview (May 1963)

ARMAGEDDON

"And they assembled them in that place which is called in Hebrew Armageddon": The scene of a final battle between the forces of good and evil, prophesied in the Bible (Revelation 16) to occur at the end of the world.

The war of Armageddon has already started. . . . God is using nature as one of his many weapons. He is sending hurricanes so fast that they [the enemy, the white devils] can't name them. He is drowning them in floods and causing their cars to crash and their airplanes cannot stay up in the sky. Their boats are sinking because Allah controls all things and he is using all methods to begin to wipe the devils off the planet, [and] the enemy is dying of diseases that have never been so deadly.

—Malcolm, reported in FBI file (January 31, 1965)

AUDUBON BALLROOM, HARLEM. Scene of Malcolm's assassination at the opening of a public rally on February 21, 1965.

Outside the Audubon Ballroom in Harlem, just before the assassination of Malcolm X, February 21, 1965.

UPI/Bettmann

UPI/Bettmann

Outside the Audubon Ballroom just after the assassination; Malcolm X on stretcher.

THE AUTOBIOGRAPHY OF MALCOLM X. Now a modern American classic; written by Malcolm with Alex Haley in 1963–1964, it was published in 1965, after the assassination.

Malcolm X in 1965.   Author Alex Haley in 1977.

AWARDS

i

I've received an award. Whenever I walk the street and see people ready to get with it, that's my reward. Whenever people come out, they know in advance what I'm going to talk about, and if they show any sign of interest in it or agreement with it, that's my reward. And when they show that they're fed up with this slow pace [of the civil rights movement], that's my reward.

—Malcolm, interview with Claude Lewis (December 1964)

ii

He [Martin Luther King, Jr.] got the peace prize, and *we* got the problem.

—Malcolm, interview with Claude Lewis (December 1964)

Dr. and Mrs. Martin Luther King, Jr., at Nobel Peace Prize celebration on December 17, 1964. *The Bettmann Archive*

B

B

BACK TO AFRICA

The twenty-two million so-called Negroes should be separated completely from America and should be permitted to go back home to our African homeland, which is a long-range program. So the short-range program is that we must eat while we're still here, we must have a place to sleep, we must have clothes to wear, we must have better jobs, we must have better education. So that although our long-range political philosophy is to migrate back to our African homeland, our short-range program must involve that which is necessary to enable us to live a better life while we are still here.

—Malcolm, interview with A.B. Spellman (March 1964)

BALLOTS OR BULLETS

Independence comes only by two ways—by ballots or bullets. Historically you'll find that everyone who gets freedom gets it through ballots or bullets. Now naturally everyone prefers ballots, and even I prefer ballots, but I don't discount bullets. I'm not interested in either ballots or bullets; I'm interested in freedom.

—Malcolm, interview with Claude Lewis (December 1964)

BEARDS

i

The Subject [Malcolm] wears chin whiskers.

—FBI file (May 4, 1953)

Malcolm X in Africa in 1964.

Schomburg Center for Research in Black Culture

ii

Malcolm and I were the first to start growing a beard; he had started when he was in Africa, and he came back and I had a beard, so we were both laughing about it. In Islam at that time [1964], Black Muslims had skinny heads, clean faces, and they started to say he and I were losing our minds.

—Charles Kenyatta remembers

18

I might leave it [the beard] on forever, or I might shave it off in the morning. I'm not dogmatic about anything. I don't intend to get into any more straitjackets.

—Malcolm, interview with Claude Lewis (December 1964)

Malcolm was *the bravest man* I've ever known because he said things that no one else was saying. I remember my father saying to me this man is not brave, he is crazy. To stand up and say these things to white people and talk about the President—he is a mad man. But before Malcolm died my father accepted him too, as did many, many other blacks, and so did whites, because he was a brave and thoughtful man. [He gave] people words to hold on to. If he said some obstreperous things, they were, I think, all part of the grand design.

—Claude Lewis remembers

Malcolm was *the brightest light* we produced in the twentieth century, and when he was gone our movement was set back a generation.

—John Henrik Clarke remembers

C

CHARITY

We were going to Bridgeport one night and this man came up, obviously a person who begs for money to buy something to drink, you know, wine or something, and he said, "Mr. X, could you give me fifty cents so I could get a bowl of bean soup?" Because at that time fifty cents could buy a big bowl of bean soup and a big piece of corn bread, or an even bigger bottle of wine. So he gave the guy fifty cents, right? So we were sitting in the car. Now we [Muslims] don't support wine habits; we don't give people money to buy alcohol, wine, or drugs and all that, so everybody was quiet. Nobody's talking; nobody's saying, "Brother Minister, why did you give the man the fifty cents? You know the man is not going to buy any food with that money." Nobody said anything. Then all of a sudden he said, after about twenty blocks on our way to Bridgeport, "I know what you're thinking," and we said we aren't thinking anything, and he said, "Yes, you are; and I don't know if that man is really hungry, if he really wants something to eat or something to drink, but had I not given him the fifty cents, it would have been on my conscience that perhaps the man was hungry, and I couldn't allow a person to be hungry if I could afford to feed that person." And he started teaching us about charity. He taught us about charity all the way to Bridgeport, Connecticut.

—Benjamin Karim remembers

CIVIL RIGHTS

THE BILL

I don't think the Civil Rights Bill has anything to do with integration. The Civil Rights Bill, in my opinion, is that which is supposed to put everyone in this country, including twenty-two million black people, in a position to get what the country is [supposed to be] offering everyone in this country. Civil rights doesn't mean that I have to go and push my way into some white man's house or some white man's neighborhood or some white man's school. Civil rights means that I am supposed to have the equality of opportunity to do whatever my particular talent will allow me, as long as I am not stepping on someone's toes or breaking the law.

—Malcolm, panel with Louis Lomax (April 1964)

The Bettmann Archive

Journalist and author Louis Lomax.

The local civil rights leaders are usually involved right in the midst of the situation. They see it as it is, and they realize that it takes a combination of groups to attack the problem most effectively. Also, most local civil rights leaders have more independence of action, and usually they are more in tune and in touch with the people. But the national leaders of the civil rights movement are out of touch with the problem, and usually they are paid leaders. . . . They are full-time leaders, they are professional leaders, and whoever pays their salary has a great say-so in what they do and what they don't do.

—Malcolm, interview with A.B. Spellman (March 1964)

Civil Rights leaders at convention of the American Society of Newspaper Editors, April 16, 1974. *Left to right*: Whitney Young of the National Urban League; Roy Wilkins of the National Association for the Advancement of Colored People (NAACP), James Farmer of the Congress of Racial Equality (CORE), and John Lewis of the Student Nonviolent Coordinating Committee (SNCC).

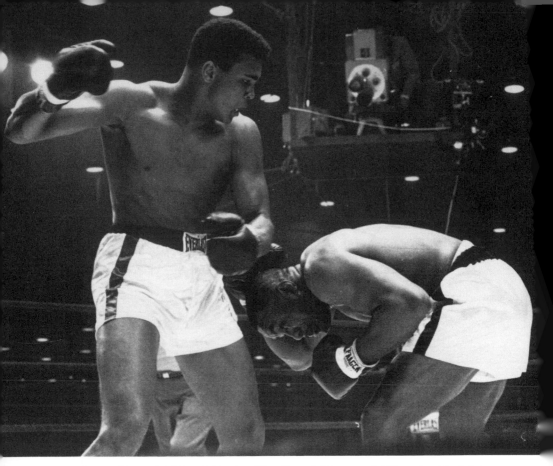

Sonny Liston (*right*) and Cassius Clay (later Muhammad Ali) at the title fight on February 25, 1964; Clay won the championship with a technical knockout in the seventh round. *UPI/Bettmann*

CLAY, CASSIUS (MUHAMMAD ALI)

Cassius wasn't going to have it without Malcolm being there [in Miami, for the world heavyweight boxing championship title match with Sonny Liston, February 1964], and Malcolm was there. Malcolm called me before the fight and said it was sure to be one of the greatest upsets in modern times, or something like that. And afterwards he called me back, and you could hear all this whooping and hollering going on in the background of the dressing room. Malcolm could not have been higher in his life than when he and Cassius Clay were so close as they were. And then they fell out. When Malcolm was ejected from the Nation of Islam, Cassius Clay stayed with the Messenger, Mr. Muhammad.

—Alex Haley remembers

COFFEE

They were very courteous, very polite [at Harvard University]. They had prepared a huge dinner for Malcolm, but Muslims only eat one meal a day, and Malcolm told them, "I've eaten for the day; I only eat one meal a day, so I can't have anything to eat, but I will have ice cream and coffee."

And they said, "Would you like some milk in your coffee?"

And he said, "Yes, that's the only thing I like integrated."

—Robert Haggins remembers

COLUMBUS, CHRISTOPHER

Here's a man who discovered absolutely nothing. He got lost. He was looking for India and made a mistake. . . . Columbus landed on this island, San Salvador, and he told the people, "I have discovered you in the name of the Queen of Spain." Which is the most ridiculous thing I've ever heard. How can you discover a human being? Somebody's about to have dinner and you intrude; [you sit down and they share their meal with you,] then you stand up and say, "I discover you! You are now discovered; you are Indian." They must have looked at each other wondering, like, where did this fool come from.

—Malcolm, as remembered by Robert Haggins

The landing of Columbus, after the painting by Vanderlyne.

D

❖❖❖ D ❖❖❖

DANGER

I have to face this alone. . . . They are out to kill me. I don't care about myself. I only want to protect my family and the OAAU [Organization of Afro-American Unity]. No matter what happens to me personally, it is important that the OAAU continues to exist, do you understand that?

Tommy X, marching at the Unity Funeral Home where Malcolm's body was on view, February 1965. *UPI/Bettmann*

. . . I'm no stranger to danger. I have lived with danger all my life. I never expect to die of old age. I know that I have done the very best that I could for our people. . . . As I told you when we first began, after I was expelled from the Black Muslims, I did not want an organization that depended on the life of one man. The organization must be able to survive on its own.

—Malcolm, as remembered by Earl Grant

DEATH AND DYING

i

Malcolm talked often about the possibility of him being killed and he was very candid about it. He expected to be killed. The unsettling thing for him was that he never knew when it was going to come—the next month or that year. He kept saying, "I have a lot to get done, a lot of things to tie together, to bring together, because the movement will go on long after I am gone."

—Claude Lewis remembers

ii

He would speak of these death threats; he would say, "Brother, I don't think I'm going to live to read this book [The Autobiography of Malcolm X] in print."

—Alex Haley remembers

A Ku Klux Klan cross-burning in Stone Mountain, Georgia.

iii

I don't take anything lightly. I don't take life lightly. But I never worry about dying. I don't see how a Negro can worry about dying at this late date. But I think that Negro organizations that talk about killing other Negroes should first go and talk to somebody about practicing some of their killing skill on the Ku Klux Klan and the White Citizens Council.

—Malcolm, interview with Claude Lewis (December 1964)

DECOLONIZATION

. . . What interested Malcolm first was the decoloniza-
tion of the black mind—the wakening of a proud, bold, de-
manding new consciousness of color and everything color
means in white America.

Malcolm pursued this end with utter reckless-
ness. . . . His genius was attack, for which he offered no
apology beyond the argument that a program was pointless
until the slumbering black masses were wakened to their
need for one.

—Peter Goldman (1979)

DESEGREGATION

i

The Thirteenth and Fourteenth Amendments were other
acts by white liberals that didn't solve our problems because
if they were enacted in sincerity, we wouldn't have the problems today. Then you have nine more hypocrites posing as
Supreme Court justices; [they] came up with the so-called
desegregation decision in 1954, which was nothing but a doctrine of hypocrisy because those judges, who were masters of
the English language and phraseology, if they really wanted
the black man to be desegregated in this country, would have
worded that decision [in a way that] would have made it
impossible for the crackers in the South to sidestep it.

—Malcolm, WUST interview (May 1963)

ii

The Supreme Court decision has never been enforced. Desegregation has never taken place. The promises have never been fulfilled. We have received only tokens, substitutes, trickery, and deceit.✓

—Malcolm, the <u>Playboy</u> interview (May 1963)

On the steps of the Supreme Court in Washington, D.C., May 5, 1954, following the landmark desegregation case of Brown v. Board of Education.

UPI/Bettmann

DETROIT RED/BIG RED. Malcolm's street names in New York and Boston, where he thrived in his late teens by pushing dope, playing the numbers, peddling bootleg whiskey, and hustling. Actually Malcolm had grown up not in Detroit but in the East Lansing area of Michigan.

Schomburg Center for Research in Black Culture

Malcolm Little, age fifteen.

A DOLL FOR ATTALLAH

One day I happened to come upon the fact that the next day was his eldest daughter Attallah's birthday, and I just knew Malcolm, as busy as he was and as guilty as he was about not spending much time with his family and what not, I just knew he'd forgot. So that afternoon I went uptown and I bought a large brown doll with all kinds of little frou-frou around her frock, with ruffles and frills and so forth, and I put it into a closet. And Malcolm came that night and we had our regular interview, and when he was getting ready to leave, I said sort of quietly, "You know, Brother Malcolm, I was just happening to be looking at my notes and I noticed that tomorrow is the birthday for Attallah, and I know as busy as you are you simply haven't had time to stop and pick her up something. I knew you'd want to, so I got this for you." And then I handed him the doll. That was as close as I ever saw Malcolm come to tears, as he took the doll. He didn't say much of anything, but I knew he was deeply moved. And then he went on out.

—Alex Haley remembers

Author Alex Haley in 1976.

UPI/Bettmann

E

◆◆◆ E ◆◆◆

EACH ONE TEACH ONE!! A motto for Muslims, from a letter written by Malcolm from Charlestown (Massachusetts) state prison, 1952.

EAST ELMHURST, QUEENS. Malcolm's residence after January 1958; his house here was firebombed February 14, 1965, one week before his death.

Malcolm X at his house in Queens after it was firebombed, February 14, 1965.

UPI/Bettmann

EDUCATION

i

Malcolm had no formal Ph.D.; he had a Ph.D. in Malcolmism, he had a Ph.D. in Americanism, in what had gone wrong with this country, and he brought it to you; and for the first time many of us began to look at ourselves again, and to say, "Hold it, it's possible to get an education and not sell your soul. It's possible to work at a job and not demean yourself; it's possible to walk upright like a human being." . . . He taught me, and I'm sure a number of others, that you are indeed worthy of being on this planet earth.

—Sonia Sanchez remembers

ii

The black college student will be very instrumental in the liberation of black people in this country.

—Malcolm, as remembered by Benjamin Karim

EISENHOWER, DWIGHT D., U.S. PRESIDENT 1953–1961

We wrote to Ike and asked him to come and help us, and what did he do? He had to play golf.

.   .   .

President Eisenhower gets ready for a round of golf in Palm Springs, California, in 1960. *UPI/Bettmann*

Eisenhower has a caddy he calls Cemetery. The name is quite appropriate because that Negro is mentally dead.

—Malcolm, reported in FBI file (April 30, 1958)

EMANCIPATION PROCLAMATION

The Emancipation Proclamation wasn't designed to free the Negro. If it was, we would be free. We wouldn't still be around here begging for civil rights.

—Malcolm, WUST interview (May 1963)

F

He really was *a family man.* In other circumstances, if racism and other kinds of cruelties were not operating against him, he would have been the typical family man, having the job and looking after the wife and children and being a religious man—that is really who Malcolm was. I think in the best of all possible worlds Malcolm would have been a preacher and a teacher and a family man, but under the circumstances he was forced to become the public political activist, and he had enough courage to become that.

—Maya Angelou remembers

Malcolm X with his daughter, Ilysah, at Kennedy Airport, on his return from the Middle East in May 1964.

FARRAKHAN, LOUIS

i

[One person that Malcolm] highly respected was a young fellow who had been a folk singer or a popular singer [Gene Louis Walcott], and he had become a member of the Nation of Islam and was very popular and well-liked. Malcolm called him "my little brother," and they were most fond of each other. And this young man was Louis Farrakhan, as he is known today, and I think that is what he was termed then, although he was probably called Louis X or a number of Xes—I don't know how many—but that is one person he was really close to. And he was very proud of being the big brother, so to speak, of little brother Farrakhan.

—Alex Haley remembers

Louis Farrakhan surrounded by bodyguards at a rally in 1985.

ii

When Farrakhan was sent to [his ministry in] Boston he didn't even have shoes or food for his family, and Malcolm gave Farrakhan shoes for his feet and food for his family. He had quite a bit of love for Farrakhan, and it actually physically grieved Malcolm when Farrakhan began speaking out against him. I have never seen Malcolm care about what anyone said about him. Except Farrakhan.

—Benjamin Karim remembers

❖❖❖ G ❖❖❖

GETTING EVEN

Hundreds of kids were involved in boycotts in the South, and they were being hit by police and hosed down, and the dogs were set on them. . . . I was young myself, and it just seemed like nobody was defending these kids. And I remember Malcolm using the analogy of a snake. If a snake bites your child, he said, you don't go out looking for that particular snake; you go out looking for any snake that you can see, because any snake has the same potential as the snake that bit your child.

—Kathryn Gibson remembers

Malcolm X at a Harlem rally in 1963; he protests the violence against peaceful demonstrators in Birmingham, Alabama.

GROWING UP

I was born in Omaha on May 19, 1925. My light color is the result of my mother's mother having been raped by a white man. . . . My father was a militant follower of Marcus Garvey's "Back to Africa" movement. The Lansing, Michigan, equivalent of the Ku Klux Klan warned him to stop preaching Garvey's message, but he kept on and one of my earliest memories is of being snatched awake one night with a lot of screaming going on because our home was afire. But my father got louder about Garvey, and the next time he was found bludgeoned in the head, lying across streetcar tracks. He died soon and our family was in a bad way. We were so hungry we were dizzy and we had nowhere to turn. Finally the authorities came in and we children were scattered about in different places as public wards. I happened to become the ward of a white couple who ran a correctional school for white boys. This family liked me in the way they liked their house pets. They got me enrolled in an all-white school. I was popular, I played sports and everything, and studied hard, and I stayed at the head of my class through the eighth grade. That summer I was fourteen, but I was big enough to get away with telling a lie that I was twenty-one, so I got a job working in the dining car of a train that ran between Boston and New York City.

On my layovers in New York I'd go to Harlem. That's where I saw in the bars all these men and women with what looked like the easiest life in the world. Plenty of money, big cars, all of it. I could tell they were in the rackets and vice. I hung around these bars whenever I came in town, and I kept my ears and eyes open and my mouth shut. And they kept their eyes on me, too. Finally, one day a numbers man told me that he needed a runner, and I never caught the night train back to Boston. Right there was when I started my life in crime. I was in all of it that the white police and the gangsters left open to the black criminal. I was in numbers, bootleg liquor, "hot" goods, women. I sold the bodies of black women to white men. I was in dope, I was in everything evil you could name. The only thing I could say for myself was that I did not indulge in hitting anybody over the head.

—Malcolm, the Playboy interview (May 1963)

H

✧✧✧ H ✧✧✧

HATE

The thing that Malcolm hated most was ignorance.

—Benjamin Karim remembers

"THE HATE THAT HATE PRODUCED." The five-part report by Mike Wallace, televised in July 1959, that brought the Black Muslim movement—and Malcolm X—to the attention of the American public.

Radio and television news personality Mike Wallace in 1955.

THE HINTON JOHNSON INCIDENT. The arrest of Black Muslim Hinton Johnson, after he had been severely beaten by the police, on April 17, 1957, that prompted an angry demonstration, led by Malcolm X, at the 123rd Street precinct in Harlem; the incident significantly widened Malcolm's popularity among New York blacks.

THE HONORABLE ELIJAH MUHAMMAD

i

[The government] should subsidize him. He's cleaning up the mess white men have made. He's saving the government millions of dollars, taking black men off welfare, showing them how to do something for themselves. . . . Messenger Muhammad restores our love for our own kind, which enables us to work together in unity and harmony. He shows us how to pool our financial resources and our talents. . . .

Elijah Muhammad in 1961. *UPI/Bettmann Newsphotos*

We are taught by Mr. Muhammad that it is very important to improve the black man's economy, and his thrift. But to do this, we must have land of our own. The brainwashed black man can never learn to stand on his own two feet until he is on his own.

—Malcolm, the Playboy interview (May 1963)

ii

Mr. Muhammad says that Allah is going to wake up all black men to see the white man as he really is and see what Christianity has done to them. The Honorable Elijah Muhammad doesn't teach hate. The white man isn't important enough for the Honorable Elijah Muhammad and his followers to spend any time hating him.

—Malcolm, the Playboy interview (May 1963)

AP/Wide World Photo

The Hotel Theresa.

THE HOTEL THERESA. The hotel at 125th Street and Seventh Avenue, in Harlem, where Malcolm headquartered his Muslim Mosque, Inc.

HUMAN RIGHTS

i

It is not a problem of civil rights but a problem of human rights.

—Malcolm, public statement (July 17, 1964)

ii

My stand is the same as that of twenty-two million so-called Negroes. . . . Our people want a complete freedom, justice, and equality; [we want] recognition and respect as human beings. That's the objective of every black man in this country. Some think that integration will bring it about. There are others who think that separation will bring it about. So integration is not the objective, nor is separation the objective. The objective is complete respect—recognition and respect as a human being.

—Malcolm, panel with Louis Lomax (April 1964)

HYPOCRISY

i

We [Muslims] are against the white man in America because of his enslavement of our people and his oppression of our people and his exploitation of our people and his continued hypocrisy, his refusal to stop doing this. [He uses] his forked tongue to make the world think that he is getting better, when all he has done is allow us to advance from ancient slavery to modern slavery.

—Malcolm, WUST interview (May 1963)

ii

This is an era of hypocrisy. . . . When white folks pretend that they want Negroes to be free, and Negroes pretend to white folks that they really believe that white folks want them to be free, [that's] an era of hypocrisy, brother. You fool me and I fool you; you pretend that you're my brother and I pretend that I really believe you believe you're my brother.

—Malcolm, interview with Claude Lewis (December 1964)

iii

A man who tosses worms into the river isn't necessarily a friend of the fish. All the fish who take him for a friend . . . usually end up in the frying pan.✓

—Malcolm, the Playboy interview (May 1963)

I

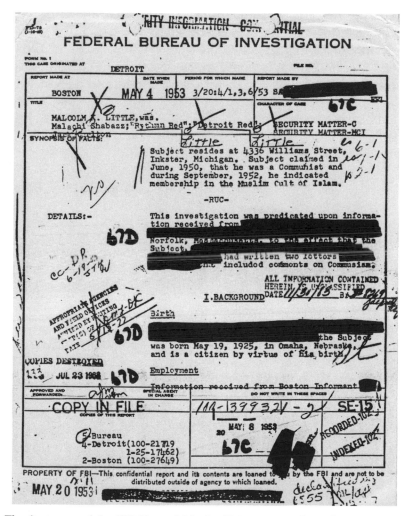

I HAVE ALWAYS BEEN A COMMUNIST. A statement by Malcolm, from a letter written in prison on June 29, 1950.

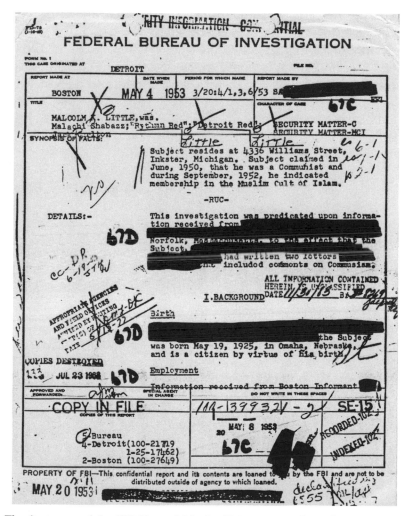

The first page of the FBI file on Malcolm X; it reports a letter he wrote in 1950 stating he was a communist.

INTEGRATION

I don't see how you could call the strides being made in the field of integration rapid when you don't have one city in this country that can honestly say it is an example of sincere integration. The first city to integrate was Washington, D.C., and it has become, because of integration, the only city in the country, according to government statistics, which has a majority population of so-called Negroes. Which shows you that when the black people come in, the white men run out, and the white liberals run out faster than the white conservatives. The white northerners run out more swiftly than the white southerners, so we just don't see where integration has worked in any city north, south, east, or west. It is only a very hypothetical approach to the problem.

—Malcolm, WUST interview (May 1963)

What was accomplished [by the integration of James Meredith into the University of Mississippi]? It took fifteen thousand troops to put Meredith in the University of Mississippi. Those troops and three million dollars—that's what was spent—to get one Negro in. That three million dollars could have been used much more wisely by the federal government to elevate the living standards of all the Negroes in Mississippi.

—Malcolm, the Playboy interview (May 1963)

INTERMARRIAGE

I believe in recognizing every human being as a human being, neither white, black, brown, nor red. When you are dealing with humanity as one family, there's no question of integration or intermarriage. It's just one human being marrying another human being or one human being living with another human being. I may say, though, that I don't think the burden to defend any such position should ever be put upon the black man. Because it is the white man collectively who has shown that he is hostile towards integration and towards intermarriage and towards other strides towards oneness.

—Malcolm, interview with Pierre Berton (January 1965)

J

J

JEWS

The followers of Mr. Muhammad aren't anti-anything but anti-wrong, anti-exploitation, and anti-oppression. A lot of the Jews have a guilty conscience when you mention exploitation because they realize they control ninety percent of the businesses in every Negro community from the Atlantic to the Pacific and that they get more benefit from the Negro's purchasing power than the Negro himself does or than any other segment of the white community does, so they have a guilt complex on this. And whenever you mention exploitation of Negroes, most Jews think that you're talking about them, and in order to hide what they are guilty of, they accuse you of being anti-Semitic.

—Malcolm, interview with Kenneth Clark (June 1963)

K

❖❖❖ K ❖❖❖

KENNEDY, JOHN FITZGERALD, U.S. PRESIDENT 1961–1963

i
He was one of the shrewdest backfield runners that history has ever recorded.

—Malcolm, public address (February 14, 1965)
in reference to the Kennedy administration's
policy of "benevolent colonialism" in Africa

UIPI/Bettmann

President John F. Kennedy in 1962.

President John F. Kennedy's casket in the memorial procession to Arlington National Cemetery on November 25, 1963.

ii

At a rally held by the NOI in New York City on December 1, 1963, [Malcolm] stated that the late President Kennedy "never foresaw that the chickens would come home to roost so soon. . . . Being an old farm boy myself, chickens coming home to roost never did make me sad; they always made me glad."

Elijah Muhammad, national leader of the NOI, was scheduled to speak at this New York rally but canceled his appearance out of respect to the death of President Kennedy and instructed NOI members to make no comments concerning the assassination of the President.

—FBI file (December 6, 1963)

KU KLUX KLAN

A cowardly outfit.

—Malcolm, public address (February 14, 1965)

A Ku Klux Klan gathering in New Jersey. *UPI/Bettmann*

L

L

LEGACY

Malcolm [became] an authentic folk hero for blacks, and it was they to whom he primarily addressed himself. His supreme gift to them was that he loved them, that he believed in their possibilities and tried to make them believe too.

—Peter Goldman (1979)

The memorial service for Malcolm X on February 27, 1965; Ossie Davis addresses the congregation. *UPI/Bettmann*

Outside the memorial service; the overflow from the chapel lines the streets.

LINCOLN, ABRAHAM,
U.S. PRESIDENT 1861–1865

Lincoln was a hypocrite who wasn't interested in freeing the black people. He was posing as a liberal. He was interested in saving the Union and he said that if he could keep them slaves and save the Union, he would keep them slaves, and if he had to let them go to save the Union, he would let them go. . . . He was interested in perpetuating the power of the white man.

—Malcolm, WUST interview (May 1963)

LITTLE. Malcolm's family name; his father, Earl Little, was a Baptist preacher from Georgia.

LOVE

i
Mr. Muhammad teaches us to love each other, and when I say love each other, [I mean] love our own kind. This is all black people need to be taught in this country.

—Malcolm, interview with Kenneth Clark (June 1963)

ii
Messenger Muhammad teaches us to love for our brother what we love for ourselves, but we must first know who our brother is and who is not our brother.

—Malcolm, Los Angeles Herald Dispatch (July 18, 1957)

iii
Malcolm considered himself to be the spiritual property of the people who produced him. He did not consider himself to be their savior, he was far too modest for that, and gave that role to another; but he considered himself to be their servant and, in order not to betray their trust, he was willing to die, and died. . . . What made him unfamiliar and dangerous was not his hatred for white people but his love for blacks, his apprehension of the horror of the black condition and the reasons for it, and his determination so to work on their hearts and minds that they would be enabled to see their condition and change it themselves.

—James Baldwin (April 1972)

Malcolm X giving press conference at the National Memorial African Book Store in New York, March 1964.

LOVES

What Malcolm loved most were truth, knowledge—I mean knowledge just for the sake of knowledge—and teaching. And he loved his family, of course.

—Benjamin Karim remembers

M

THE MARCH ON WASHINGTON. The massive civil rights demonstration in the nation's capital on August 28, 1963, which was, Malcolm commented, "run by whites in front of a statue of a president [Lincoln] who has been dead for a hundred years and who didn't like us when he was alive."

A view of the March on Washington from the steps of the Lincoln Memorial.

Aerial view of the Lincoln Memorial during the March on Washington.

MARTIN AND MALCOLM

i

You don't have to criticize Reverend Martin Luther King, Jr. His actions criticize him. . . .

Any Negro who teaches other Negroes to turn the other cheek in the face of attack is disarming that Negro of his God-given right, of his moral right, of his natural right, of his intelligent right to defend himself. Everything in nature can

Dr. Martin Luther King and Malcolm X on the only occasion they met face to face, in the U.S. Capitol on March 24, 1964.

Schomburg Center for Research in Black Culture

defend itself, and is right in defending itself, except the American Negro. And men like King. . . . He doesn't tell them [Negroes], "Don't fight each other." "Don't fight the white man" is what he's saying in essence, because the followers of Martin Luther King, Jr., will cut each other from head to foot, but they will not do anything to defend themselves against the attacks of the white man. . . .

White people follow King. *White* people pay King. *White* people subsidize King. *White* people support King. But the masses of black people don't support Martin Luther King, Jr. King is the best weapon that the white man, who wants to brutalize Negroes, has ever gotten in this country, because he is setting up a situation where, when the white man wants to attack Negroes, they can't defend themselves. ✓

—Malcolm, interview with Kenneth Clark (June 1963)

ii

I know Malcolm had contempt for Martin King. After King's ["I Have a Dream"] speech in the March on Washington, which I missed—I was in jail at the time—Malcolm said that King's dream was a nightmare, only he's too dumb to know it.

—James Farmer remembers

iii

Everytime I hear Martin's got a dream, I think Negro leaders have to come out of the clouds and wake up and stop dreaming and start facing reality. ✓

—Malcolm, interview with Claude Lewis (December 1964)

iv

Dr. King wants the same thing I want—freedom. Now his method of going about getting it is the nonviolent way. We may differ in method, but that does not mean we differ in objective.

—Malcolm, panel with Louis Lomax (April 1964)

v

I don't think that any black person can speak of Malcolm and Martin without wishing that they were here. It is not possible for me to speak of them without a sense of loss and grief and rage; and with the sense, furthermore, of having been forced to undergo an unforgivable indignity, both personal and vast. Our children need them, which is, indeed, the reason that they are not here; and now we, the blacks, must make certain that our children never forget them.

James Baldwin (April 197?)

MECCA

The holiest and most sacred city on earth. The fountain of truth, love, peace, and brotherhood.

—Malcolm, a postcard to Dick Schaap (April 1964)

MMI/MUSLIM MOSQUE, INC. The black nationalist organization founded by Malcolm on March 12, 1964, after his split with Elijah Muhammad and the NOI, to provide a religious, cultural, and moral base for members of the black community in Harlem.

MUSLIMS

Muslims are not a hate group. We're not bitter toward the white man; in fact, I believe that we Muslims who follow Mr. Elijah Muhammad get along better with white people than the Christian Negroes . . . who profess to love white people. In fact, most white people recognize us Muslims and respect us for what we are, just as we respect them. . . . They don't have any trouble out of us; we don't have any trouble out of them.

—Malcolm, interview with William Kunstler (March 1960)

N

❖❖❖ N ❖❖❖

A *NEW WORLD ORDER* IS IN THE MAKING, AND IT IS UP TO US TO PREPARE OURSELVES THAT WE MAY TAKE OUR RIGHTFUL PLACE IN IT. Malcolm, from a letter written in 1956 to an NOI brother.

NEWS MEDIA

i

White reporters do nothing but distort what is said or take it out of context or blow up what they consider to be negative. They don't come [to the mosque] to listen objectively and then go out and report objectively; they go out to project us as a racist group, as a black supremacist group, or as a group advocating violence. . . .

If they want to cover our meetings, let them get someone black who looks like us to come in and cover our meetings. . . . I heard that one television network is flying a Negro in all the way from New York City just to cover this meeting because we won't let the white reporters in, and this means that this particular network, which is one of the largest in the country, here in this city, the capital, doesn't even have one Negro in this city working for them.

—Malcolm, WUST interview (May 1963)

Malcolm X speaking to reporters in Washington, May 1963.

ii

Malcolm was good at manipulating the press. He knew how to use the press; he charmed the press and provided it with material. He was exciting. He probably never had quite the following that he liked to imply he had, but most political leaders don't have quite the following they imply they have.

—Dick Schaap remembers

iii

The media's the most powerful entity on earth. . . . They have the power to make the innocent guilty and to make the guilty innocent, and that's power. Because they control the minds of the masses.√

—Malcolm, as remembered by Robert Haggins

NOI/NATION OF ISLAM

I was in prison and I was an atheist. In fact, one of the persons who started me to thinking seriously was an atheist—a Negro inmate . . . who switched my reading habits in the direction away from fiction to nonfiction, so that by the time one of my brothers [who had become a Muslim in Detroit] told me about Islam, I was open-minded and I began to read in that direction. One of the things that appealed to me was in Islam a man is honored as a human being and not measured by the color of his skin.

—Malcolm, interview with Robert Penn Warren (1964)

Malcolm X protesting arrest of black Muslims in Rochester (NY) at Harlem rally in 1963.

BELIEFS

We believe in God. We believe in justice. We believe in freedom. We believe in equality. And we believe that God, our God, our Supreme Being, whose proper name is Allah, will execute judgment and justice in whatever way he sees fit against the people who are guilty of this crime against our people in this country.

—Malcolm, interview with Richard Elman (May 1962)

DOCTRINE

The Muslim doctrine could be summed up and often was summed up by Elijah Muhammad as, quote, "to tell you the truth about the white man and to tell you the truth about yourself; only when you know these two truths can you ever be free and can you ever obtain justice or equality."

—C. Eric Lincoln remembers

LIFESTYLE

We ate only once a day. . . . Our diet changed; where we ate white bread we were told to eat wheat bread, what a lot of people now call health food. Movies were cut out. Parties were cut out. We had a juke box that only played jazz and Middle Eastern music or music from Africa—no blues, perhaps because a lot of blues is sad and a lot is talking about my woman left me or I caught somebody with her, or something like that.

—Benjamin Karim remembers

MORALITY

We must stop drinking, we must stop smoking, we must stop committing fornication and adultery, we must stop gambling and cheating and using profanity, we must stop showing disrespect for our women, we must reform ourselves as parents so we can set the proper example for our children. Once we reform ourselves of these immoral habits, that makes us more godly, more godlike, more righteous. That means we are qualified, then, to be on God's side, and it puts God on our side. God becomes our champion. . . ✓

—Malcolm, interview with Kenneth Clark (June 1963)

POLICY

[The Honorable Elijah Muhammad teaches] complete separation, not only physical separation but moral separation. ✓

—Malcolm, interview with Kenneth Clark (June 1963)

Mr. Muhammad teaches us to be for what's really practical—that's separation. It's more natural than integration.

—Malcolm, the Playboy interview (May 1963)

Elijah Muhammad opening the National Convention of Black Muslims on February 26, 1966.

NONVIOLENCE

i

Look right now what's going on in and around Saigon and Hanoi and in the Congo and elsewhere. They [the American government] are violent when their interests are at stake. . . . They're violent in Korea, they're violent in Germany, they're violent in the South Pacific, they're violent wherever they go. But when it comes time for you and me to protect ourselves against lynchings, they tell us to be nonviolent.

—Malcolm, public address (February 14, 1965)

ii

I think that if there's going to be a flowing of blood, it should be reciprocal. Black people shouldn't be willing to bleed unless white people are willing to bleed. And black people shouldn't be willing to be nonviolent unless white people are going to be nonviolent.

—Malcolm, interview with Claude Lewis (December 1964)

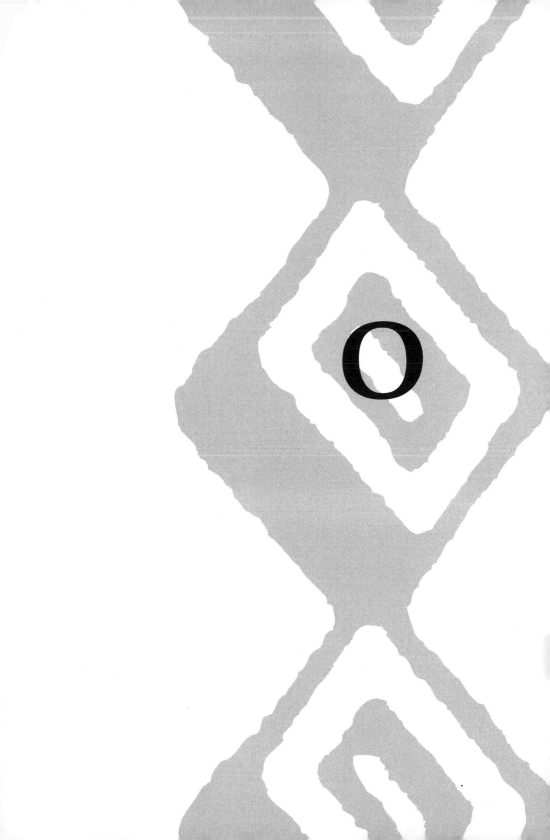

$\diamond\!\!\diamond\!\!\diamond$ O $\diamond\!\!\diamond\!\!\diamond$

OAAU/ORGANIZATION OF AFRO-AMERICAN UNITY. Established by Malcolm on June 28, 1964; the *Omaha World-Herald* reported the organization's commitment to doing "whatever is necessary to bring the Negro struggle from the level of civil rights to the level of human rights."

OMAHA, NEBRASKA. The birthplace of Malcolm K. Little, May 19, 1925.

ORATORY

i

Malcolm could speak for hours and I never saw him use a note. And he never lost track of his point, even though people would jump up and yell [and talk back]. It was like the Baptist church . . . where you respond back to the minister, and as he is speaking you say "yes" or "make it plain" or "teach," and people did that constantly and . . . it just sort of kept on pumping him and kept him going. He was so very dynamic; I don't know anyone who equals him, I really don't.

—Kathryn Gibson remembers

When Malcolm strolled to the microphone there was a radiant intensity—he may have stood in a spotlight, I don't know, but radiant was certainly the impression I got—and then he started his delivery. He spoke of our origins; he said that he came to us in the name of all that is eternal—the black

Malcolm X as minister in the Nation of Islam.

man and said that before you are an American you're black, before you were a Republican you were black, before you were a Democrat you were black, and it was just extraordinary. The audience just erupted . . . viscerally, powerfully.

—Michael Thelwell remembers

iii

[When] the speech came together, it was vintage Malcolm. . . . "Someone slaps you on one cheek and you're going to turn the other?" he roared, attacking the idiocy of nonviolence. "You've seen it on TV. You've seen those firehoses rolling black women down the street! The skirts flying! You've seen the police dogs turned loose on little black children, biting their flesh and tearing their clothes!" And then he roared again, "Don't let those dogs bite those children! Kill the damn dogs!" Everybody in the audience rose to their feet in applause . . . and most of them were white. Not many speakers could [improvise] a speech like that, could start from scratch and come through the way he did. He came through like a champion, which he was.

—James Farmer remembers

OXFORD UNION DEBATE. December 3, 1964; a major address in which Malcolm defended the use of extremism and "any means necessary" in the struggle of black Americans for human liberty.

P

POSTCARDS FROM MECCA

I had gotten two postcards from him, from Mecca, on his two separate trips there. . . . The first card had said: "Dear Brother James, I am now in Mecca, the most beautiful and sacred city in the world, where I have witnessed pilgrims of all colors worshipping Allah in perfect peace and harmony and brotherhood such as I have never seen in the States." The second card [was signed Malik El-Shabazz and read]: "Here I am, back in Mecca. I am still traveling, trying to broaden my mind, for I've seen too much of the damage narrow-minded-ness can make of things, and when I return home to America, I will devote what energies I have to repairing the damage."

When I asked him if that indicated a change in his thinking, he said yes, as a matter of fact, it did. . . . "I had believed everything the Honorable Elijah Muhammad had told us, and the Honorable Elijah Muhammad had told us that Islam was a black man's religion—exclusively—and that the blue-eyed devils could not get close to Mecca, that they would be killed if they tried to enter that sacred city. In Mecca I saw blue-eyed blonds worshipping Allah just as I was, kneeling right beside me, so obviously the Honorable Elijah Muhammad had lied."

—James Farmer remembers

PRIDE

i

Malcolm made blacks feel good about them-
selves. . . . I remember clearly in those days people trying
to bleach their skin and straighten their hair; Malcolm said
that was wrong, [that we should] love Mother Africa. Here
was a guy who made black people feel good about their thick
lips and their hair, which used to be called nappy, and he
allowed them to have self-esteem and convinced them that
they had power, they had authority, and that they were not
minorities if you looked at it from a world perspective.

—Claude Lewis remembers

ii

Malcolm stirred the imaginations of all blacks. . . . He
stirred them to go back to their yearnings, [to say,] "I want to
be a lawyer, a doctor, an Indian chief, but I also want to have
my dignity." And he was saying it's possible. [Even if you
had had] the experience [of an] educational system that
hounded you, that said, "Yes, you have a degree, but you're
inferior; yes, you're a doctor, but you're still a nigger." [Mal-
colm said,] "I can tell you how not to be a nigger in this
country."

—Sonia Sanchez remembers

Malcolm X's message is heard. *UPI/Bettmann*

PRISONS AND CHRISTIANS

No Muslims go to prison. Those men [Muslims in Lorton Reformatory] weren't Muslims before they went to prison. . . . They were Christians before they went to prison, Baptists, Methodists, Catholics, [and their religion] led them into a life of crime; and the inability of that religion to reform them of their criminal tendencies is what made them wind up in prison. After getting into prison they heard about the teachings of the Honorable Elijah Muhammad, and then became Muslims, then reformed themselves, and were then rehabilitated and changed, and became better men. The Christian psychologists, the Christian theologists, were unable to reform these men and rehabilitate these men.

—Malcolm, WUST interview (May 1963)

He was *the protector.* It was like you knew you had a big brother at home who could knock down anybody who messed with you.

—Kathryn Gibson remembers

Q

QUEST

i

Malcolm X was a man in motion, he was a seeker. . . .
He was trying, as it were, to locate the truth. . . .

—Robert Penn Warren (December 1966)

ii

Malcolm had no loyalty to misconceptions. He was intelligent and courageous enough to admit when a position no longer held true. . . . Most people would rather like to say what they say they believe in and then repeat themselves instead of saying, "I'm not in love with this position; I'm in love with the search for truth." And that was Malcolm.

—Maya Angelou remembers

QUESTIONS

"Don't you believe there are any good white people?" asked a white coed who had followed Malcolm from her college in New England to the Muslim restaurant in Harlem. Malcolm answered, "People's *deeds* I believe in, Miss—not their words."

"What can I do?" she then demanded. "Nothing," he replied.

$\diamond\!\diamond\!\diamond$ R $\diamond\!\diamond\!\diamond$

RACISM

i
To me [a racial extremist] is extreme in his desire and in his love and in his devotion to his race. From that angle, it's not a crime to be a racial extremist. Catholics say that the Catholic church is the only church and the only way to get to heaven. Baptists say that no one can go to heaven unless they're baptized. And Jews themselves for thousands of years have taught that they alone are God's chosen people. . . . [Nonetheless,] the Catholics have never been accused of advocating Catholic supremacy and the Jews are not accused of advocating Jewish supremacy, nor are they accused of teaching race hatred. [Furthermore, since the Bible] promises that non-Christians will be destroyed in a fiery death someday by God Himself, I find it difficult that Catholics and Christians accuse us of teaching racial supremacy or racial hatred, because their own history and their own teachings are filled with it.

—Malcolm, interview with William Kunstler (March 1960)

ii
Once I was a racist, yes. But now I have turned my direction away from anything that's racist.

—Malcolm, interview with Robert Penn Warren (1964)

Malcolm was not a racist, not even when he thought he was. His intelligence was more complex than that.

—Peter Goldman (1979)

Malcolm X making a point.

RADICAL STUFF

In Malcolm's day a guy standing up on television saying white folks are the devil and are going to suffer the wrath of

Allah, and it's going to be bad; saying that your cities will burn, and that black people do not or may not want the company of white people and that we reject you, that we want power over our own communities and we don't want integration or, as Malcolm put it, "coffee with a cracker"; saying that black people have a worth and pride and history of their own—I mean, that was radical stuff then. It was revolutionary.

—Peter Goldman remembers

RAGE

i

Malcolm was the crazy nigger gone public; he undertook to carry Harlem's fury downtown, to tell white people to their faces in their own mass media, what ordinary blacks had been saying about them backstairs for all these years. He did not "teach" hate or need to; he exploited a vein of hate that was there already and to which few black Americans were totally immune. . . .

Malcolm saw and exploited the uses of rage as an organizing principle.

—Peter Goldman (1979)

ii

Malcolm was saying out loud what African Americans had been saying all along behind closed doors, but he was willing to say it out loud, and in that way he was willing to release blacks from the fear that had enveloped them for so many years, because he was saying it on TV and all over the streets of Harlem.

—Sonia Sanchez remembers

RIOTERS

You can't call a man defending his home a rioter. You can't call a man who is defending his babies and his children

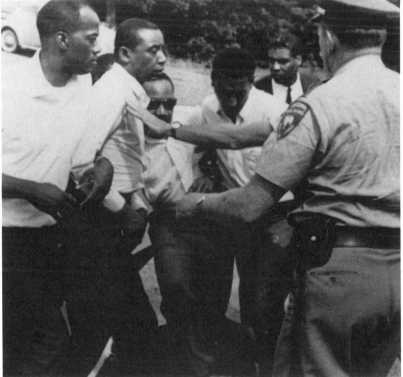

Police disrupting civil disobedience action led by Dr. Martin Luther King (wearing glasses).

and his women a rioter. You call the rioter the one who is attacking—those white people down there [in Birmingham], who are policemen in uniform. The law itself is what is attacking our people and that law in Alabama could never attack black people unless the federal government of the United States condoned it.

—Malcolm, WUST interview (May 1963)

THE RONALD STOKES INCIDENT. The fatal shooting of Muslim brother Ronald Stokes in police gunfire at the Los Angeles mosque on the night of April 17, 1962; in response to an alarm, the police squad had converged erroneously at the mosque, and six other brothers were also wounded. Malcolm conducted the funeral services for Stokes.

S

SEGREGATION

Segregation is that which is forced upon inferiors by superiors. Separation is done voluntarily by two equals. . . . The Negro schools in the Negro community are controlled by whites; the businesses in the Negro community are controlled by whites; the economy of the Negro community is controlled by whites. And since the Negro society or community is controlled or regulated by outsiders, it is a segregated community. . . . Muslims who follow the Honorable Elijah Muhammad are as much against segregation as we are against integration. We are against segregation because it is unjust and we are against integration because its hypothesis is a false solution to a real problem.

—Malcolm, WUST interview (May 1963)

A newly desegregated bus in Montgomery, Alabama, in December 1956; a black woman still takes her seat in the back.

Betty Shabazz, Malcolm X's widow, leaving the city morgue,
February 22, 1965.

SHABAZZ, BETTY

She's the only person I'd trust with my life.

—Malcolm, as remembered by Alex Haley

SHABAZZ, TRIBE OF

A way has been made that we [the followers of Elijah Muhammad] will be able to escape the destruction [of Armageddon] and return to the East, where all black people will live and you will be the rulers of the planet. You are the descendants of the moon people and are from the tribe of Shabazz. Your home is in the East . . . but only the righteous will be taken.

—Malcolm, reported in FBI file (January 31, 1956)

SINCERITY

i

In whatever I did or do, even if I made mistakes, they were made in sincerity. If I'm wrong, I'm wrong in sincerity. . . . [A person] can be *wrong*, but if he's sincere you can put up with him. But you can't put up with a person who's *right* if he's insincere. I'd rather deal with a person's sincerity, and respect a person for their sincerity, than anything else.

—Malcolm, interview with Claude Lewis (December 1964)

ii

My sincerity is my best credential.

—Malcolm, interview with Joe Rainey (March 1964)

Malcolm X in front of the Connecticut state capitol building.

THE SPLIT

i

Malcolm's popularity outside the Nation [of Islam] was the main factor for the split with Elijah Muhammad. But the jealousy and envy had roots. . . . At that time the Muslims had built quite a few businesses—very lucrative ones—and had even bought a jet, a jet plane. There was a lot of money floating around and a lot of people were spending money in areas where it shouldn't have been spent, and Malcolm spoke out against it. And they knew that if Mr. Muhammad passed on [he was seriously ill at the time], they would not have their positions anymore, because they were the first people that Malcolm would have gotten rid of. . . . They had gotten greedy.

—Benjamin Karim remembers

ii

I did encounter opposition within the Nation of Islam. Many obstacles were placed in my path, not by the Honorable Elijah Muhammad but by others who were around him, and since I believe that his analysis of the race problem is the best one and his solution is the only one, I felt that I could circumvent these obstacles and expedite his program better by remaining out of the Nation of Islam and establishing a Muslim group [the MMI], which is an action group designed to eliminate the same ills that the teachings of the Honorable Elijah Muhammad have made so manifest in this country.

—Malcolm, interview with A.B. Spellman (March 1964)

T

T

Malcolm was *the tallest tree* in the forest.

—Robert Haggins remembers

TEMPLE NO. 7. Also called Mosque No. 7 (after December 1961) and located on the third floor at 102 West 116th Street, corner of Lenox. The Nation of Islam met here at 2:00 p.m. every Sunday and at 8:00 p.m. Wednesdays and Fridays; Malcolm served as minister from June 1954 until his split with Elijah Muhammad in March 1964.

Malcolm speaks at a Harlem rally in 1963; police watch from roof of building across the way. *UPI/Bettmann*

TIGERS AND TOOTHPICKS

In another time and in another place Malcolm could have been a king; he could have made a nation and he could have destroyed a nation. And the nation that destroyed him with such a unique ruthlessness destroyed him for a reason, and no other nation would have done it quite the same way. He was in a crossfire in a power struggle in the twentieth century, and there was no way he could have survived it without having equal competing power, and he didn't have it. When you rise to face a tiger, you can't do it with a toothpick.

—John Henrik Clarke remembers

U

U

UMWAELZUNG

People involved in a revolution don't become part of the system; they destroy the system, they change the system. The genuine word for a revolution is *Umwaelzung*, which means a complete overturning and a complete change. The Negro revolution is no revolution because it condemns the system and then asks the system that it has condemned to accept them into their system.

—Malcolm, interview with A.B. Spellman (May 1964)

UNCLES

And then along came the Muslim movement and frightened the white man so hard that he began to say, "Thank God for old Uncle Roy [Wilkins, executive secretary of the NAACP], and Uncle Whitney [Young, chief of the National Urban League], and Uncle A. Philip [Randolph, socialist and civil rights activist], and Uncle—" You've got a whole lot of uncles in there; I can't remember their names, [but] they're all older than I, so I call them uncle. Plus, if you use the word "Uncle Tom" nowadays, I hear they can sue you for libel. So I don't call any of them Uncle Tom anymore; I call them Uncle Roy.

·   —Malcolm, public address (February 14, 1965)

Civil rights leaders meeting in New York 1964. *Left to right*: Bayard Rustin, Jack Greenberg, Whitney Young, James Farmer, Roy Wilkins, Dr. Martin Luther King, John Lewis, A. Philip Randolph and Courtland Cox.

V

V

VICTORIES

[Martin Luther] King had to be measured by his victories. But what King did, what the NAACP did, what the March on Washington did, what Whitney Young did, what Roy Wilkins did, all that was for the benefit of the southern Negro. There were no obtainable, immediate results for the northern ghettoized black, whose housing is getting worse; who is unable to find work; whose schools are deteriorating; who sees constantly more rats and roaches and more garbage

Bayard Rustin speaking from the steps of the Lincoln Memorial at the August 28, 1963 March on Washington; he was its deputy director.

in the streets. He, because he is human, must find victory somewhere, and he finds his victory within. He needed Malcolm, who brought him an internal victory, precisely because the external victory was beyond his reach. What can bring satisfaction is the feeling that he is black, he is a man, he is internally free. King had to win victories in the real world. Malcolm's were the kind you can create yourself.

—Bayard Rustin, with Peter Goldman (1973)

W

W

WHATEVER IS NECESSARY

I propose that we have the right to do whatever is necessary to bring about an answer to our problem. . . . If it's necessary to leave to get a solution, then we should leave. If we can get a solution by staying here, then we should stay. The main thing we want is a solution.

.   .   .

I'm for the freedom of the twenty-two million Afro-Americans *by any means necessary. By any means necessary!* I'm for freedom. I'm for a society in which our people are recognized and respected as human beings, and I believe that we have the right to resort to *any means necessary* to bring that about.

—Malcolm, interview with Claude Lewis (December 1964)

WHITE MEN/WHITE DEVILS

i

A devil is still a devil whether he wears a bed sheet or a Brooks Brothers suit.

—Malcolm, the Playboy interview (May 1963)

ii

We Muslims believe that the white race, which is guilty of having oppressed and exploited and enslaved our people here in America, should and will be the victims of God's divine wrath.

—Malcolm, the Playboy interview (May 1963)

iii

What I want to know is how the white man, with the blood of black people dripping off his fingers, can have the audacity to be asking black people do they hate him. That takes a lot of nerve.

—Malcolm, the Playboy interview (May 1963)

UPI/Bettmann

A white mob at a lynching of two blacks accused of murder and assault on two white teenagers in Indiana, August 1930.

151

iv

[Malcolm] was the black man who looked the white man in the eye and forgave nothing.

—Robert Penn Warren (December 1966)

Malcolm X: the unwavering, unforgiving stare.

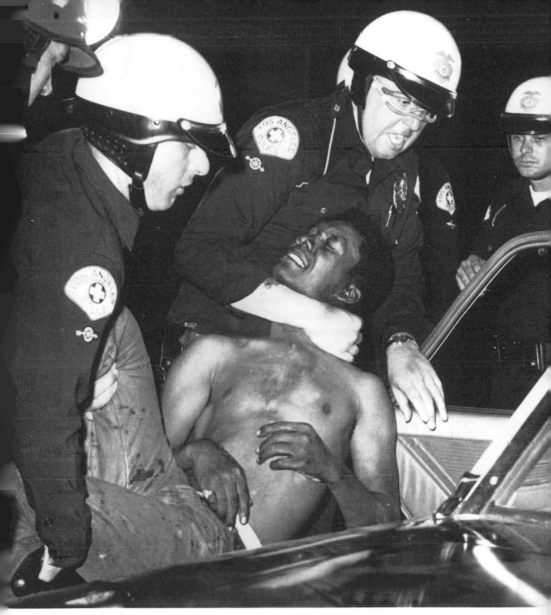

Riot police in Los Angeles, August 13, 1965. *UPI/Bettmann*

v

The white race is doomed not *because* it's white, but because of its misdeeds.

—Malcolm, interview with Robert Penn Warren (1964)

vi

I'm not blanketly condemning all whites. All of them
don't oppress. All of them aren't in a position to. But most of
them are, and most of them do∨

—Malcolm, a public rally (June 1964)

vii

[Malcolm's] challenge [to the white man] was to prove
that you are as great as you say you are, that you are as moral
as you say you are, that you are as kind as you say you are,
that you are as loving as you say you are, that you are as
altruistic as you say you are, that you are as *superior* as you
say you are.

—C. Eric Lincoln, with Peter Goldman (1973)

Malcolm was *a witness for the prosecution* against white America—a "field nigger," he called himself, giving incendiary voice to the discontents of our urban black under-class. Everything about Malcolm was an accusation.

—Peter Goldman (1979)

Malcolm X observing Albany legislature in action, January 1965.

X

I went to the Muslim restaurant on 116th Street and Lenox Avenue, and I had been sitting there for about five minutes when this tall gentleman with a briefcase came in. His entourage following him, he came over to my table and said, "Are you Mr. Haggins? I'm Malcolm X."

"Fine," I said, and pulled out my pad to begin our interview. "What is your last name?" I said.

And he said, "That's it, X."

And I said, "How did you get a name like X? X must be an initial. What is the whole name? What is the rest?"

He said, "You want me to give you my slave name?"

"Slave name?" I said.

And he said, "Yes. I dropped my slave name. That name was Malcolm Little, but I don't carry a slave name anymore. I carry X. I carry X because I don't know my real last name."

Then we started talking about how we got our names and how ridiculous it was for me or any black person to carry the name of Haggins or any other English or Irish or white person's name and how people were bought and slaved like cattle and their names changed to reflect who owned them. I had never had anybody awaken me like that before in my life. . . .

I was ready for Malcolm. I didn't know it at first, but I was.

—Robert Haggins remembers

X STANDS FOR THE UNKNOWN. A statement by Malcolm in an interview on WUST, May 1963.